HAMSTER CARE

THE ESSENTIAL GUIDE TO OWNERSHIP, CARE, & TRAINING FOR YOUR PET

Kate H. Pellham

© 2015

DISCLAIMER

TABLE OF CONTENTS

INTRODUCTION

Are you considering getting a pet hamster for yourself or your children? Do you already own a hamster and want to learn more about it to make sure you are giving it everything it needs? Well with this comprehensive guide to hamster care, you'll learn everything you need to know about your pet hamster.

Not all hamsters are the same, in fact, there are over 25 different species of hamster, each one with its own unique characteristics and needs. Of this 25, only 5 of them are commonly kept as pets.

If you aren't sure that a pet hamster is the right choice for you, this guide will help you decide. It will teach you about the 5 common domesticated breeds including how their characteristics and needs differ, ensuring that you not only know how to take the best possible care of your pet, but that you also pick the species that suits you best.

Owning a pet is a big responsibility, even when the pet itself is very small. You must ensure that you're feeding it the right food, providing it the right amount of space to explore and also giving it the attention it needs to be the gentle and friendly pet that you want it to be.

In the subsequent chapters you will learn:

- The daily lifestyle of wild hamsters
- The physical and behavioral characteristics of the 5 species of pet hamster
- A pet hamster's basic needs
- Everything you need to know about keeping a hamster as a pet
- How to take the best care of your hamster
- How to train your hamster to do some cool tricks
- Instructions for breeding hamsters

So, if you want to learn everything you could ever need to know about owning a pet hamster, keep reading!

Chapter 1 - The Physical & Behavioral Traits of Hamsters

The hamster family is made up of over 25 different species, the majority of which are not actually kept as pets. This chapter will focus on the 5 species of hamster that are most commonly kept as pets.

The two most popular breeds in the United States are the Golden hamster and the Campbell's dwarf hamster.

- Golden Hamster (Mesocricetus Auratus)

The Golden hamster is native to Northern Syria and Southern Turkey. The number of wild golden hamsters has declined significantly over the years, to the point that they are actually now considered vulnerable to extinction, as their preferred habitat is being lost to agriculture and industrialization.

The number of domesticated Golden hamsters however is growing rapidly helped by the fact that they are regularly used in scientific research, and are also the most popular breed of pet hamster.

Adult hamsters are between 5 to 7 inches long and live for about 3 years. They also reproduce extremely rapidly. A female hamster becomes fertile every 4 days, and the gestation period (the time from fertilization and birth) lasts only 16 days. Litters consist of an average of between 8 and 10 newborn pups.

For this reason, it's highly recommended that you avoid getting hamsters of the opposite sex. If you put a male and female in a cage together, you'll end up with hundreds of hamsters within a few months. So unless you intend to breed, stick with one hamster, or two hamsters of the same sex.

The Golden hamster gets its name from the coloring of its fur as it is a blend of black, brown and gold, however as a result of breeding; there are now a number of different fur colorations available so the name "golden" is now no longer always appropriate. For example, you can now get golden hamsters with cream, blonde, black, copper, tortoiseshell (black and gold) and difference shades of gray fur.

Breeders have also produced golden hamsters with longer hair than their wild counterparts. Typically these are called Angora hamsters, or "teddy bear" hamsters. The males have longer hair that creates a sort of "skirt" of fur around its lower backside, however the females of this breed still have short hair, but it is more velvety.

In terms of behavior, golden hamsters are some of the most docile and mild-mannered hamsters available.

They are also famous for their drinking habit. In the wild, golden hamsters collect and store fruits throughout the summer to survive throughout the winter, however by the time winter arrives, those fruits have fermented and become alcoholic.

Because of this, golden hamsters have developed a taste for alcohol and their livers are *five times* larger than you would expect for their body size, meaning that they could beat anyone in a drinking competition.

- Campbell's Dwarf Hamster (Phodopus Campbell)

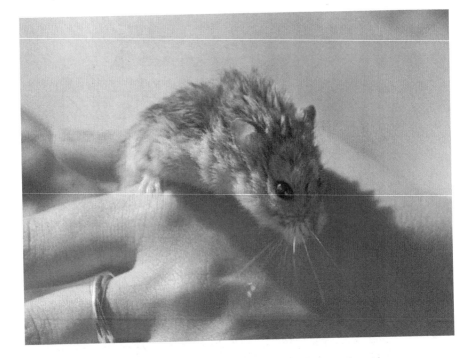

Native to China, Mongolia, Kazakhstan and Russia, the Campbell's dwarf hamster is growing in popularity as a pet mainly because their small size makes them extra adorable. In the wild, they average about 3 inches however the domesticated versions are a little larger since they are fed a more nutritious diet more regularly.

The underside of the hamster, from the tail up to the jaw, is covered with a coat of cream-colored fur, whilst the upper side is a light or dark grey with a long black, or dark grey stripe, running from the tip of its nose, down to its tail. They have a shorter lifespan (ranging from just 1 to 2 years) and have a high risk of cancer than the Golden hamster. They are also at greater risk of having a genetic mutation which prevents them from being able to digest carbohydrates or fats. This results in them therefore technically being omnivores. It is really important that you monitor your hamster regularly to ensure it is properly digesting fruits and fatty foods. If it isn't, you'll need to restrict its diet primarily to insects and other low carbohydrate, low-fat foods. You'll learn more about this in Chapter 4.

Like many other kinds of rodents, the teeth of a dwarf hamster continue to grow throughout its entire life. This means that they need smooth, nontoxic wood to chew on in order to keep their teeth filed down.

In captivity, females can reproduce as many as 18 litters a year, with an average of 6 pups per litter. They can also be bred with the Djungarian Russian dwarf hamster to create a hybrid however this hybrid species is prone to a lot of health problems, so this type of crossbreeding is not recommended.

They are less docile than the Golden hamster but they can still be great pets if cared for well. You will therefore need to give them more attention and spend more time with them so that they get used to you. You should also avoid putting your hand directly into the cage to pick it up, as they are extremely territorial. Try instead using a spoon that it can climb on to.

- Djungarian Russian Dwarf Hamster (Phodopus Sungorus)

The Djungarian Russian dwarf hamster is often confused with the Campbell's dwarf hamster because they are similar in size and color. They can also be bred together, although as mentioned above this is not recommended for health reasons.

While there are a lot of similarities, the Djungarian Russian dwarf hamster is a unique species. It can be slightly larger at 3 to 4 inches in length. In the wild, it has a full solid gray coat, instead of the half white/half gray pattern of the Campbell's dwarf hamster, however it does have the dark stripe running down its back.

Their fur coats change throughout the year, in the summer they are the darker coloration described above, and their coat is thinner. In the winter however their dark coat is replaced by a thick coat of pearly white fur. This does not always happen when kept in captivity since the change is triggered by changes in daylight and temperature, which may not be as dramatic when the hamster constantly lives indoors.

Domesticated breeds can have a variety of different color patterns including a year round summer coat (the darker coloration); a year-round winter coat (the pearly white); or a blend of the two resulting in an appearance similar to the Campbell's dwarf hamster.

If you are interested in breeding hamsters, this species may be your best bet as the females become pregnant again immediately after giving birth, literally on the same day.

They are a little less territorial than the Campbell's dwarf hamster which therefore makes them easier to tame. They do however need more attention and human contact than other hamsters and are generally much faster than other breeds, making them harder to handle. For these reasons, they are not the best option for young children.

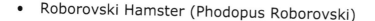

- Roborovski Hamster (Phodopus Roborovski)

This species of hamster is originally native to the desert climates in Kazakhstan, Mongolia and China. They are actually smaller than both species of dwarf hamster at just 2 inches long, and in terms of physical appearance there are 10 distinct color variations.

The most common variety is the "agouti" which is white on the underside with light brown, grayish fur on top. It also has distinctive white spots above the eyes that look like eyebrows.

These are one of the more active hamsters, with studies confirming that they run an average of 100 miles per night, that's almost 4 full-length marathons before the sun comes up. They are also more social and prefer to live with other fellow Roborovski hamsters. Remember, if you want to avoid being overrun with tiny hamsters, make sure any hamsters you keep together are of the same sex.

They are naturally extremely shy so avoid loud noises or sudden movements. It's best to get them at a young age so that they can become accustomed to you. They do not bite as much as some breeds of hamster however when interacting with them; allow them to be the boss so that they don't become scared.

Over the years they have evolved to be active at dawn and dusk, this is known as "crepuscular" so it's best to avoid bright lights. You can use red lights in or near their cage if you want to look at them because their eyes are not capable of seeing red light so you won't disturb them.

- Chinese Hamster (Cricetulus Griseus)

Like the Roborovski, the Chinese hamster is native to the deserts of China and Mongolia, however they are a bit larger at an average of 4 inches in length.

They appear longer and thinner than other hamsters and also have the longest tails. In the wild their fur is mostly brown with a black stripe running down its back, and flecks of black and gray throughout, their belly is usually a little whiter. They are sometimes confused with mice since their build and coloration is very similar.

In captivity they have been bred into 3 variations; the wild coloration described above, an all-white variety with black eyes and a light gray variety with a darker stripe running down its back.

They can initially be unfriendly and skittish but once tamed they are extremely gentle and calm, and enjoy clinging to your finger with all four paws. Like the Roborovski, they are very quick and agile which means they need a larger cage with plenty of toys and equipment so that they can stay active.

Because they are thinner, they can also escape through the bars of most hamster cages so something with solid walls is required. If you want to keep more than one in a cage, it must be big enough for each of them to have plenty of their own space. You should also introduce them at a young age since the Chinese hamster is not as social or friendly as other species can be.

After reading through these descriptions, you should now have a better idea of what it might be like to own each of these varieties as a pet. In the next chapter you'll learn more practical information about keeping hamsters as pets, including the advantages and disadvantages, and what your responsibilities as an owner would be.

CHAPTER 2 - HAMSTERS AS PETS

Keeping hamsters as pets can either be the best or worst choice for you depending on your situation. As with any pet, it's important to take the time to do the research, so that you can be sure you are making the right decision for both you and your new pet's happiness.

In this chapter, we'll detail some of the advantages and disadvantages of keeping a hamster as a pet. Read through them carefully and consider your own situation, this will help you work out whether or not a hamster is the right choice for you.

- The Pros of Keeping a Hamster as a Pet

    - Low Maintenance

    Hamsters are one of the easiest pets to take care of. They rank up there with fish in that department but they are much cuter and cuddlier than any fish will ever be. You really only need to make sure your hamster is fed and clean. They are also pretty solitary animals so if you don't have the time to give them a lot of attention, they will still fare much better than a cat or dog would if they were ignored. Do however keep in mind that if you don't take them out of the cage at least once per day to play with them, they will not become socialized which means they will treat you like a stranger. The more time you invest in your hamster, the more social and friendly they will become. On the other hand, if you mostly want a pet to look at, you don't need to take the time to socialize them, just keep them fed and clean and make sure they have toys and a running wheel to exercise with.

    - Really Cute

You probably don't need to be convinced that hamsters are cute. If you are reading this guide and considering buying one then you already know that. They are small, fluffy and adorable. The best part is they stay that way their entire life. This is perfect for those who like the idea of buying a kitten or puppy, but don't want them to grow out of their cute baby phase. Hamsters stay small, fluffy and cute for the whole of their lives and will always fit into the palm of your hand. Some species will even fit on your finger. So if you're looking for a pet that will always be small and cute, a hamster is your best bet. Plus, you can even dress it up in tiny hats and jackets for added cuteness!

- Great for Small Spaces

Dogs need a big yard and cats need at least a big enough house to explore, particularly if they are indoor cats. Hamster conversely can be contained in a small cage which means you can keep one as a pet even if you live in a small studio apartment. It's also the perfect pet if you rent a room in a shared apartment as you can keep a pet hamster in your room without disturbing anyone else in the house. This makes hamsters a great alternative to cats or dogs if your home has limited space. It's also ideal because any mess created by a hamster will be contained in its cage.

- Affordable

As far as pets go, a hamster is one of the most affordable choices you could make. The hamster itself is relatively cheap and the supplies it needs are very basic and inexpensive. Its diet of seeds, nuts, fruits and vegetables is also easy to accomplish, and you therefore don't need to purchase any highly specialized foods. You can buy prepared hamster food at pet stores, but it's actually better to feed them fresh seeds, leafy vegetables and the occasional piece of fruit. Bedding can also be bought however it can also be made up of old newspapers that you would otherwise have thrown out. In fact; newspapers make better bedding than the store bought stuff. Most of your expenses are going to be the initial investment; buying the hamster, the cage and the other basic supplies. After that, your maintenance costs will be much lower than they would be for almost all other pets.

- Great Alternative for People with Allergies

If you are allergic to cats and dogs but miss having a furry friend at home, a hamster could be a good option for you. They are not hypoallergenic but because their habitat is contained in a small space and not spread throughout the house (as it is with cats or dogs), it won't trigger serious allergic reactions. This also makes it a great compromise if some members of the household want a pet but others are allergic. You can have the best of both worlds; an adorable furry friend and no risk of allergic reaction.

- Low Commitment

If you are interested in the fun and benefits of having a pet but not so interested in committing to the responsibility for a full decade or longer, then the hamster is your new best friend. They have relatively short life spans ranging from 1 to 4 years, so you can provide it with a full and happy life for the time it's here, and it will then die naturally before you have a chance to get bored of it. It's a good choice for those who aren't sure they can commit to caring for another creature for a long period of time.

– Good Starter Pet

Because hamsters are a short term commitment and also low maintenance, they are a good pet to get if you have never owned one before. This does not however necessarily mean that they are perfect for young children, typically in fact it's not recommended that children under the age of 10 are given sole responsibility for any pet. If you do however decide that you want to teach your child how to care for a pet, a hamster is a good choice, but you will need to supervise and make sure the hamster is getting what it needs at all time; just as you would with any pet. Hamsters also don't require house training or being taken for walks.

– Decrease stress, depression and anxiety

Studies have shown that owning a pet helps with stress, depression and anxiety. In one study, patients who spent a short time with a dog before going into surgery or getting a difficult treatment, had 37% lower stress levels than the patients who didn't spend any time with a dog beforehand. The reason owning a pet (including a hamster) has such a powerful effect on your mental health, is because the pleasure you get from interacting with a pet and caring for another life, reduces the stress hormones in your body and releases oxytocin into your brain (one of the neurotransmitters that cause you to feel happy). In order to get these benefits, you should play with your hamster at least once or twice a day.

- The Cons of Keeping a Hamster as a Pet

   – Responsibility

While hamsters are a low maintenance pet, there is still some maintenance involved. You need to give them fresh food and water daily and you need to clean out their cage at least once per week. You also need to keep an eye out for signs of certain illnesses. This is not a lot in comparison to other pets but it's still something that you need to do in order to keep your hamster happy and healthy. If one of your main concerns about getting a pet is that you don't have any time for it, then you really need to consider whether or not you will have the time to take care of your hamster's basic needs.

- Smell

Hamsters can get a bit smelly. This is especially the case if you don't clean out their cage regularly. The females also start to have a stronger smell when they are in heat (which happens every 4 days) since they are releasing stronger pheromones in order to attract a mate. The smell can easily be managed and is also contained to wherever your hamster is and not spread through the whole house. It's however still worth mentioning, as some people are extremely sensitive to smell. You can reduce this smell further by simply cleaning the cage twice per week instead of just once. If your sensitivity to smells is very high, you may want to hold off on getting any sort of pet.

- Can Sometimes Be Aggressive

The golden hamster is one of the most docile and gentle species of hamster so if you're worried about biting, this is the one to get. Other species are a little more aggressive by nature, however all hamsters will bite if they feel threatened by something or surprised by someone that they do not know. This means that if you don't have the time to take your hamster out of the cage and play with it at least once or twice every day, you might have to deal with occasional biting. You need to socialize thoroughly your hamster and make sure that it knows you and your scent, so that it doesn't feel threatened when you hold it. For the best results, you should try to get your hamster when it is as young as possible, as it's harder to socialize an adult than a pup.

- Owning More than One Is Difficult

If you only want to get one hamster then this is not a problem you'll need to worry about, but if you were hoping to have 2 or more hamsters, you're going to run into problems. First of all, if the hamsters are of the opposite sex, you will quickly end up with dozens of baby hamsters on your hands. As you learned in the previous chapter, they reproduce very frequently and very quickly; this isn't however the only problem you will have when owning more than one hamster.

Hamsters are naturally very territorial and don't usually get along with other hamsters, there is therefore a good chance you would have to keep each hamster in its own cage. You can try to introduce cautiously two hamsters to each other and see if they get along in the same cage, but the chances are low. If you really want to have any chance of keeping two hamsters in the same cage, you'll have to buy them as young as possible. Adult hamsters are not likely to ever get along with any other adult hamsters.

- Fragile

With a dog or cat, you can play and have fun without worrying too much about hurting them. Hamsters on the other hand are pretty fragile as their bones are small and can be easily broken, and their bodies can easily be damaged. This is not much of a problem if you are a mature adult who knows how to show restraint, but if you have young children in the house, they may get too excited and inadvertently end up hurting the hamster.

This is another reason they shouldn't be given to young children as pets, unless of course you have the time to supervise and make sure that they are always gentle and careful with them.

- Short Life Span

As mentioned earlier, the short life span (1 to 4 years) of a hamster makes them a good low commitment pet. However it can also be a disadvantage if you are looking for a long term pet that can really become part of the family. If this is your case, you risk forming a strong attachment to your new pet only to have it die in a few short years.

If you're looking for a pet that will be with you for a decade or more, you should avoid the hamster and go for a cat, a dog or even a parrot instead.

- Need to Watch for Certain Illnesses

This is especially the case if you have a hybrid or sibling breed, which are at a high risk for genetic disorders and other problems. Even healthy, non-hybrid species of hamster are at a high risk for certain illnesses. The most common one is diabetes because hamsters can easily become incapable of digesting carbohydrates. While all animals have their own unique health risks, hamsters are especially susceptible to certain illnesses, whereas cats & dogs are far more resilient.

Later in the book you'll learn more about how to diagnose and treat the illnesses that are most common in hamsters.

CHAPTER 3 - HAMSTER NECESSITIES

Shopping for your hamster can be simple if you know what you're looking for. If you want a specific species, it's best to go to a specialized hamster breeder rather than a pet store, where hamsters are often hybrid or sibling breed.

If you're not particularly interested in owning a specific breed, you should try checking your local animal shelter where you can usually get a hamster for free, and it often even comes with the basic supplies you require.

- The basic supplies you will need include:

    - Hamster cage; either no bars or bars. If bars, ensure they are placed close enough together so that the hamster can't squeeze through them. The cage should be a minimum of 24 square inches for a golden hamster and 19 square inches for the other breeds. Bigger is however always better for your hamster.
    - Food Dish; metal or ceramic are best. The hamster will chew through plastic.
    - Water bottle.
    - Hamster wheel; the wheel should have a solid surface (not bars or rungs). A golden hamster will need a bigger wheel than other species.
    - House; a small house is necessary so that your hamster can hide when it wants to.
    - Chew toy; hamster teeth never stop growing. Make sure there is a toy for it to chew on; otherwise it will eat through any plastic in the cage.

- There are also some non-essential but definitely beneficial items you should get:

    - Additional toys for your hamster to play with.

- Hamster ball; this should be the same dimensions as the hamster wheel, i.e. bigger for golden hamsters.
- Tubes and tunnels that attach to your cage.

Your initial investment is going to be around $100, however this includes the cage, the hamster wheel, the house, the first batch of food and (most importantly) the actual hamster. After that, any maintenance costs; more food and bedding etc, will be less than $20 per month. It can even be less if you use newspaper, toilet paper or another material instead of store-bought bedding.

Chapter 4 - The Basics of Hamster Care

In this chapter, you'll learn about the essentials of hamster care. This includes housing, feeding and keeping your hamster clean and happy. As far as pets go, hamsters are relatively low maintenance so these are good pets for people who don't have a lot of time to invest in care.

This does not however mean that you can simply buy a hamster and leave it to fend for itself. In this chapter we'll go into more details about the day to day needs of your hamster, as well as any special care that might be required if your hamster suffers from any of the common problems or illnesses that they can be prone to.

- Housing

The rule of thumb on cages is a minimum of 19 square inches per hamster; they may be small but they need a lot of space to run around and explore.

There is some debate about whether you should get a wire cage or one with solid walls. The wire cage provides better ventilation but hamsters can also chew through or escape between the bars. If you do opt for a wire cage, then make sure it's made of material that hamsters can't chew through, and that the spaces between the bars are extremely small. You shouldn't be able to fit your finger between the bars.

Inside the cage, you must have bedding. Bedding can be made of old newspaper or another similar material; alternatively you can also buy bedding from your local pet store.

Avoid cedar and pine bedding as this is not good for hamsters.

The layer of bedding should be deep enough so that the hamsters can dig into it and explore. It is usually recommended that you ensure it is always at least 3 inch deep. Each hamster should also have its own small house or place that it can safely hide. Hamsters naturally like to burrow and curl up in small spaces so providing them with deep bedding and small houses will allow them to follow happily these natural instincts.

Aside from the bedding and the small house, the cage must also contain other accessories for food, water and exercise equipment. You'll learn more about these later in this chapter.

In summary; you must make sure that the cage is big enough to hold all of these things while still giving your hamster at least 19 square inches of room to play in.

Keep your hamster's cage out of direct sunlight and avoid drafty areas (such as near doors or windows). You want to keep the temperature and environment relatively stable for your hamster so that it doesn't become distressed.

- Food & Water

Your hamster needs enough food in order to fill its cheek pouches each day. This is usually about 2 teaspoons or ½ an ounce. You should feed them at the same time each day so that your hamster knows when it will get food and doesn't become stressed out.

You have two options in terms of what you feed your hamster. You can buy prepared food pellets that contain a balance of all the nutrients a hamster needs, or provide it with fresh foods which taste better and allow your hamster to choose its favorites and balance its own diet. If you want to catch signs of diabetes and other illnesses early on, it's best to feed it a variety of fresh foods so that you can see how it handles each one.

If you go for the fresh food option, you must make sure it gets a mixture of seeds every day. In addition; feed it dark leafy greens, raw veggies and every now and again a piece of fruit. Don't feed it fruit daily as their bodies are not capable of handling very much sugar.

Make feeding time more exciting for your hamster by scattering the seeds throughout the bedding and letting your hamster hunt and dig for them. This is what they are naturally inclined to do in the wild and they will enjoy it much more than eating out of a bowl. Don't do this with moist foods (like fruits or vegetables) as it will wet the bedding.

To keep your hamster safe, **don't feed** it any of the following foods:

- unwashed fruits & vegetables (unless organic or pesticide free)
- almonds
- celery (unless chopped into very small pieces, otherwise the stringy texture can be a choking hazard)
- chocolate
- garlic
- dry kidney beans
- iceberg lettuce
- onion
- peanuts
- potato
- rhubarb
- seasoned or spicy foods
- sugary foods
- tomato leaves

They do not need much water but they should always have it available in a bottle that they can drink from. Replace the water in the bottle daily to keep it fresh. Using a water dish is not recommended because the water can quickly get dirty or the hamster may accidentally knock over the dish and therefore wet its cage.

A wet cage must always be avoided as it can quickly lead to mold, which in turn will make your hamster very sick.

- Hygiene

Your hamster can take care of its own hygiene so you don't need to bathe it. In fact trying to bathe your hamster is not recommended as it will cause your hamster a lot of stress and could result in health problems.

The cage does however need to be cleaned at least once per week, twice if you want to control the smell. To ensure you clean the cage correctly, follow the tips below:

- Remove the hamster:

Remove your hamster carefully from its cage and place it in a safe container; such as a bucket. Ensure you have put some bedding at the bottom and that the container/bucket is big enough to prevent your hamster from climbing out.

- Throw out old bedding:

Do not reuse the same bedding after cleaning the cage.

- Clean the cage:

Using warm water and a sponge or cloth, wipe the cage clean. Do not use soap unless you have purchased special soap that is safe for hamsters. Even the smallest trace of soap chemicals left on the cage can cause serious harm to your hamster, plus the cage shouldn't be totally disinfected because if it's too clean, the hamster's immune system will be lowered and it will get sick too easily.

- Clean the other items:

Clean the hamster wheel, food dish, water bottle and other items in the cage in the same way. Remember to only use warm water, no soap.

- Dry everything:

Make sure everything is completely dry before putting any new bedding in.

- Replace the bedding:

Put a 3-inch layer of fresh bedding in the bottom of the cage. Do not reuse bedding.

- Put everything back properly:

It's important to put each item back into the cage in exactly the same location it was in before you removed it. If it's moved around, your hamster will feel like it's in a whole new habitat and become quite distressed.

- Special note:

If you find a hoard of old food hidden somewhere in the cage; often inside the little house or buried in a corner, do not throw it out. Your hamster is a natural hoarder and will become distressed if it finds its stockpile is missing. Scoop it out with a spoon and set it to the side while you clean the cage.

When you're putting everything back, remember to put the food pile back exactly where you found it.

- Toys & playtime

Your hamster needs a lot of exercise, in fact as we have learned; some species can run the equivalent of 4 full marathons in a single night. If they don't have a hamster wheel or similar toys, they are going to become extremely restless and upset. This can lead to all kinds of health problems.

The one absolute necessity in every hamster cage is a wheel, so that it can run as much as it wants. Beyond that, there are all kinds of other toys available like tunnels to climb in, and little hamster jungle gyms.

Your hamster's favorite activities are running, climbing and burrowing, so keep this in mind when you are choosing it new toys.

You can also buy a hamster ball so that you can let it out to run around the house without it getting lost. Hamsters adore this as they get to exercise and explore at the same time, if you are going to do this be very careful of staircases or anything else that could harm your hamster.

If you want your hamster to be comfortable with you and with other humans in general, you should ensure that you play with it at least twice per day. If you don't do this it will get used to being on its own, which is also fine since hamsters are usually pretty solitary, but you can't have it both ways.

You either need to decide to play with your hamster every day, or leave it undisturbed to entertain itself.

- Common problems & illnesses

Wild hamsters are pretty hardy when it comes to survival but a caged habitat can cause some health problems. Here's what you need to keep an eye out for:

- Antibiotics

Many antibiotics are fatal to hamsters. Make sure the vet you visit specializes in hamsters and therefore treats them regularly.

Inexperienced vets may accidentally prescribe fatal antibiotics to hamsters.

- Cedar or Pine allergy

Hamsters cannot tolerate these types of wood, which surprisingly are quite often used in store bought cage bedding. It can cause skin problems and breathing problems.

- Hibernation

If the room temperature drops below a normal temperature, the hamster will start to hibernate. This means it will lie very still and breathe very slowly. Many owners mistakenly believe the hamster is dead or dying. Always check to see if the temperature is lower than usual before assuming your hamster is dead. Re-adjusting the temperature will be enough to wake your hamster up from hibernation.

- Skin infections

Hamsters are prone to a lot of skin problems including ringworm, mites, infected cuts/scrapes and allergic reactions. All of these need to be treated by a vet. The most obvious sign of a skin infection is excessive scratching. If you see your hamster scratching itself a lot, take it to the vet before the infection gets out of hand.

- Diarrhea

Diarrhea can be a common problem. It usually means the hamster is having trouble digesting certain foods. If you feed it a lot of fresh fruits and vegetables, hold off for a few days and stick to a diet of seeds. If the problem goes away after that, continue to avoid fresh fruits and veggies, or as a minimum only feed them to your hamster once every few days.

- Wet tail

This is fairly common especially in young hamsters but the exact cause is still unknown. It can be highly fatal so you should take your hamster to a vet as soon as you notice the symptoms. The symptoms include; diarrhea, loss of appetite, ruffled fur and lethargy.

Remember, diarrhea alone does not mean your hamster has wet tail. If its appetite and energy levels remain the same, the diarrhea is likely just to be a dietary problem and not a case of wet tail.

- Respiratory infections

This can happen a lot in hamsters. The symptoms include; sneezing, wheezing, difficulty breathing, runny eyes/nose and possible loss of appetite. If your hamster sneezes occasionally, this is not a problem, you should only take it to a vet if you notice some of the other symptoms as well.

- Abscesses

Small cuts and scrapes can become infected and fill with pus which can then lead to abscesses. This is especially common in the cheeks where rough foods can cause minor tears in the cheek lining. If you notice that your hamster looks like it constantly has food stuffed into its cheeks, take it to a vet to check for possible abscesses.

- Diabetes:

The Campbell's dwarf hamster has by far the highest risk for diabetes but it can occur in all species. If it happens, it usually presents when the hamster is between 7 to 9 months old. It is caused by; diet, stress or a dirty cage. To check for diabetes, look for signs of excessive drinking and urinating. Also check for trembling, shaking and a lower body temperature; see a vet as soon as you notice these signs. If left untreated, your hamster could fall into a coma. While there's no treatment for hamster diabetes, you can switch it to a sugar-free diet, which means no more store bought treats as these often contain corn syrup or molasses.

CHAPTER 5 - HOW TO TRAIN YOUR HAMSTER

Training your hamster is a fun way to spend time with your pet and teach it a few cool tricks that you can show off to your friends and family. You can teach hamsters to do many of the same tricks that you teach other pets like; sit, shake, roll over, play dead and so on.

Which tricks you decide to teach your hamster are totally up to you, but here are a few general guidelines that apply when trying to train your pet any trick:

- Get comfortable

In order for the training to be successful, your hamster has to be familiar with you. That means it has to know your scent and your voice. Interact with your hamster often as soon as you bring him or her home.

You should speak to your hamster a lot as well. It may seem silly to talk to an animal but it needs to get used to your voice so that when you start giving it instructions during training, it is already comfortable with it.

A great way to start building a positive relationship with your hamster is to hold it and play with it for approximately 20 minutes before you feed it. By spending quality time with your hamster immediately before meal time, it will start to make a positive association between that time with you and food. This starts to create the link you will need for your reward system to work properly during training.

The more comfortable your hamster is with you, the more quickly it will learn tricks because it will already associate you with a positive reward.

- Use rewards

Positive reinforcement is always better than negative reinforcement. Your hamster will learn the trick much more quickly with positive reinforcement. In fact you should avoid punishment as much as possible. Negative reinforcement will only make your hamster more afraid of you, and as a result it will become more difficult to teach it the more complicated tricks.

Take some time at the beginning, when your hamster is still getting used to you, to learn what its favorite treat is. Fruits and special seeds are the best options but try out different types to see which ones it seems to like best.

For the best results, the treat you use should be the same each time so that it can more easily learn that obeying commands will result in a specific special treat.

The treat should also be something that it doesn't eat on a regular basis. Don't just give it more of its regular food, instead make the treat something special that it doesn't get to eat normally. This will give the hamster extra motivation to learn tricks.

- Be consistent

For training to work, you need to be consistent in every way possible. Make time for training every day. For the best results, do it at the same time each day. The ideal time would be the evening (dusk) because this is when your hamster is most active and alert.

Use the same exact command words; these should be simple and straightforward; sit, stand, roll and so on, in conjunction with the same exact treat (as mentioned above) and the same tone of voice.

In order for your hamster to make the association between the command you give, the trick it should perform and the reward it will receive, there needs to be as much consistency as possible in your training.

At first, your hamster might not respond to commands or do tricks properly. Training takes commitment. You can't just spend one day training your hamster and expect it to be suddenly fully trained in every trick. You need to stick with it and do it over and over even when your hamster doesn't seem to be making progress. It takes time to build up those associations in your hamster's brain.

- Start simple

To make it easier on yourself and your hamster, it's best to start with the simple tricks first. Not only is it easier for you to train them but it's easier for your hamster to learn them.

For example; teaching your hamster to stand up on command is as simple as saying "stand" and holding a treat above it so that it has to stand up and reach toward it. You can also use a similar process to teach "lay down" by holding the treat below the hamster when it is standing.

Combining your commands with hand movements will also reinforce the training. It will instinctually go for the treat and will soon make the connection that following your hand results in a reward.

The other benefit of starting with these simple tricks is that you can use them to build up to more complicated tricks. For example; once you have trained your hamster to lay down on command, it will be easier to train it to roll over or play dead.

Similarly, once you have trained your hamster to stand, it will be easier to train it to jump or dance. If you were to start with more complicated tricks, your hamster might just end up feeling confused about what is going on.

- Training specific tricks

We've already given you a couple of tips for training simple tricks, like stand and lay down, here are a few suggestions for some other tricks that you can teach your hamster:

- Roll Over

  After commanding your hamster to lie down, hold the treat in front of it and spin it in circles while saying the command word "roll over." At first use your other hand to gently roll the hamster over while you do this. After a few days of rolling the hamster yourself, try saying the command (and using the circle hand motion) without rolling the hamster to see if it does it on its own. If it doesn't, continue manually rolling the hamster until it figures it out.

- Jump

  After commanding your hamster to stand up, hold the treat above its head just out of reach. Move the treat up and down above its head while saying the command word "jump." When its feet leave the floor, reward your hamster with the treat. Repeat this multiple times so that it realizes what the reward is for.

- Dance

  After commanding your hamster to stand, wave the treat above its head from side to side while saying the command word "dance." It will reach its arms from side to side for the treat. Reward it for this. Repeat this multiple times. After a few training sessions, try saying the command word without the treat in your hand. Remember to reward it if it obeys the command.

– Jumping through a Hoop

Set up a hoop and lead your hamster through it by holding a treat in front of it and having it follow your hand. Use a command word like "hoop" for this trick. Reward it each time it goes through the hoop. After multiple sessions, you can elevate the hoop off the ground and continue training the hamster to jump up and through the hoop.

– Opening a Gift

Place a treat in a small, open box and set it beside the hamster. When it removes the treat from the box, say something like "good job". Do this for a few training sessions. Then, wrap the box in shiny wrapping paper but continue to leave it open. After the hamster takes the treat from the wrapped box, say "good job" or the same positive reinforcement you used earlier. Next, place a treat inside and put a lid on the box. When the hamster removes the lid to get the treat, say "good job." After a few sessions of this, you can fully wrap the gift so that the hamster has to remove the paper to get to the treat inside. Now you can celebrate holidays with your hamster and let it open its own gifts!

CHAPTER 6 - A BRIEF GUIDE TO HAMSTER BREEDING

Breeding hamsters is actually pretty easy. In fact, it's probably harder **not** to breed hamsters. They reproduce quickly and give birth to large litters however if you are purposefully trying to breed hamsters, here are a few tips and considerations for you:

- Reproduction facts

Hamsters have one of the quickest reproductions cycles of any animal. In most species, the female goes into heat every 4 days and for some, females can become impregnated again on the same day that they give birth to a litter. The gestation period (time between impregnating and birth) lasts about 2 to 3 weeks on average.

It's important to keep in mind that a new mother might eat some of the newborn pups. This is an evolutionary survival strategy however you can minimize this risk by making sure she has plenty of food and that the conditions in her cage are as ideal as possible.

Don't worry if she does end up eating some of the pups, you can easily breed more later on.

When breeding hamsters, it is going to be more challenging for you to ensure that you don't end up with too many pups, as opposed to not enough. In the following sections of this chapter, you'll learn how to breed safely and effectively, without ending up with hundreds of little hamster pups.

- Sexing your hamster

The most basic requirement for breeding is having one male and one female hamster, this sounds simple however telling the difference between sexes is not that easy. Most pet store workers will not even know how to do it. So here is a guide to help you tell the sex of a hamster.

Pick the hamster up and hold it firmly around the middle of its body. Don't squeeze too tight but do have a firm grasp because it will squirm. Bend the body back gently and spread the bottom legs open to looking at the genital area.

On females, the genital opening and the anus will be very close together. On males, there will be a slight gap (about the size of a finger) between the genital opening and the anus. If the male is older than 5 weeks, the testicles will fall down when you hold him upright. These will appear as two pink lumps near the anus.

- Finding your hamster parents

At pet stores, many of the hamsters you find will likely be hybrids or sibling breeds (offspring of two hamsters who were siblings). You want to avoid these because they are at a high risk for genetic disorders.

It is better to get your hamsters from a breeder if you are planning to breed them yourself. A breeder will also be more knowledgeable about the hamsters and be able to determine accurately their sex. Both of these advantages are harder to find at a pet store where employees lack specialized knowledge about hamsters.

You can search for breeders online or ask your local pet store if they know of any local breeders. Don't be afraid to ask a lot of questions. You want to know as much about the hamsters as possible before you buy them.

When selecting hamsters, choose ones that have the characteristics you are looking for; that includes physical appearance and also behavior. A healthy hamster has a relatively glossy and full coat (no bald patches) and looks clean (no goop around the eyes or signs of illness).

• Introducing the breeding hamsters

With two adult hamsters that are not yet familiar with each other, you will have to be careful about introducing them to each other. When you bring your breeding hamster's home, keep them in separate containers for the night however keep their cages close to each other so that they can see and smell each other but still have their own space.

To introduce them, put the female into the male's cage. Females tend to be more territorial so they are more likely to react negatively to a new hamster in their cage. Males are generally a little more passive so this risk is lower.

When you first put them in the same cage with each other, watch them carefully to see how they get along. Make sure the male hamster has a small house he can run into if the female starts to get aggressive. If they fight a lot, put them in separate cages again.

If they don't take to each other immediately, you'll have to spend some time getting them used to each other. Put the female in the male's cage a few times a day for as long as you can without them getting overly aggressive. Keep them in separate cages overnight.

When the female goes into heat, you can put her in the male's cage again. At this point, she may be more willing to get along with the male hamster. A female hamster in heat behaves similarly to a cat. She will lie down on her stomach and raise her back end up in the air, presenting herself. She will also be more active than usual.

After they breed, allow them to spend the night in the same cage. Afterward, keep the female in a separate cage for her pregnancy and birth. In some species, the male will sometimes help during birth but there is a high risk that he will get aggressive and attack the newborn pups so it's better to keep them in separate cages during this time.

- Caring for your hamsters during pregnancy & birth

For the 2 or 3 weeks that your hamster is pregnant, she is going to eat a lot more. Make sure she gets extra food and plenty of water during this time. Otherwise, leave her alone. She will not be as playful or friendly during and immediately after pregnancy, because she's going to be more concerned about protecting the pups.

Make sure you provide the mother with nesting material while she is pregnant. Avoid the store-bought fluff because pups can get tangled up in it and choke to death or have limbs torn off. Instead, a simple sheet of plain toilet paper will work just fine. The mother will tear this into pieces to build the nest.

When she gives birth, it's going to be difficult for her but you simply have to let her go through it on her own.

If you try to help her in anyway, she'll get aggressive. Look for signs that she's going into labor.

By the time she is ready to give birth, she will be much larger than usual. It will look like she has large "saddlebags" on each side. When she starts to act restless and gathers food and nesting materials, this is the biggest sign that she is about to go into labor.

The babies will begin to come out as she is walking around the cage. She will gather them up one by one and bring them back to the nest she has prepared.

Immediately after birth, take special care not to disturb the mother or her new pups. Do not touch the pups at all. The mother will reject them if they have a foreign scent. If you absolutely need to move them, use a spoon. Rub the spoon in the sawdust or other floor material thoroughly so that it has the scent of the cage, and scoop up the pups with that to move them back into the nest.

For the first 3 weeks after birth let the mother and her pups remain totally undisturbed. Do not even try to clean the cage. Just put in food and water as necessary. Take extra care not to touch her, the pups, or anything else in the cage while you are putting in food or water. It is essential that you make sure that she has plenty of food and water as she will need more than usual of both of them while she is nursing the pups.

If you try to interfere in some way, you'll cause stress to the mother hamster that might then result in her eating the pups. You may notice her hold the pups in her mouth, this doesn't mean she's eating them. It just means she got startled and thought they might be in danger.

After 3 or 3 ½ weeks, you can handle the pups safely and separate them from the mother. Make sure to check the sex of the new pups and keep the males and females in separate cages. If you keep them all in one cage, you'll end up with sibling breeding.

- Caring for the pups

It is relatively easy to care for baby hamsters as they don't have many special needs. They do however eat a lot of food when they are young as they are still growing. Make sure there is always more than enough food in their cages so that the pups can eat their fill without having to compete with each other.

You should also make sure that the water bottle is positioned lower than usual. It must be low enough for the pups to reach it. If the water bottle leaks, be sure to clean the cage quickly. Wet cages are a huge problem for hamsters. They need a clean, dry home.

Earlier in the book we told you all about cleaning cages however if you end up having to clean the cage during the 3 week period when the mother hamster is nursing, it is essential that you are even more careful.

The rule of thumb is to leave the cage alone during this time but a wet cage is even more of a problem than disturbing the mother at this point, so you may be forced to take action.

When removing the hamsters, take care to be as gentle as possible with the mother. She will be agitated as she is being separated from her pups. When removing the pups, use a clean bowl and try to scoop up the nest along with the pups. Don't touch the inside of the bowl before using it. You should also wear gloves to avoid getting your scent on the pups.

You can leave the pups in the bowl while you clean the cage. After cleaning, remember to add new nesting material and put the pups back in first. Try to place them in the same exact spot they were in before.

After putting the pups back in, put a piece of fruit or another favorite treat for the mother in her food bowl. This will help calm her down from the stress and panic of being disturbed. Afterward, don't disturb them again. The mother may carry the pups around and relocate the nest. Just avoid interfering with her, until it's safe to remove the pups from the cage.

- Selling Your New Hamsters

Selling your hamsters can be a problem. Pet stores (especially the big chain stores) will probably not accept the hamsters and even if they do, they may not be willing to pay very much.

Your best option is to sell them individually direct to people who want to buy them. These can be your own friends and family, or you can set up an online shop. Remember to advertize well and get yourself out there. Keep your business active on social media so that you can reach as many potential buyers as possible.

One thing you'll need to consider when selling hamsters is who you want to sell them to. Many people buy hamster pups to use as snake food. If you don't want your pups to end up as food, you'll have to make sure that you price them above the cost of snake feed hamsters.

If that's not a concern for you, you'll likely see more sales if you sell them at snake feed prices. This is a matter of personal ethics that you'll have to answer for yourself.

Conclusion

Now that you have finished reading this guide, you are ready to make a smart, well-informed decision about whether or not to get a pet hamster. You know what your responsibilities will be, what supplies you need, what you need to be cautious about and how to give your pet hamster the best possible care.

Use the information in this book to choose the perfect pet hamster for you and refer to it regularly whenever you have questions or concerns about your pet. This book can be your first stop when you want to know what's going on with your hamster and what steps you need to take to help it.

Remember to consider your own situation before bringing any pet into your home. Your pet is going to become part of the family so you want to make sure it is a good fit.

For example; if you have young children, you want to make sure you choose one of the more docile and friendly species of hamster. If you don't have the time to give your hamster the attention it needs to be socialized, you'll want to choose a species that is more independent and happy to be on its own.

Don't just make an impulsive decision when you get to the store. Take the time to consider what the best option is, and plan out what you'll buy and how you'll care for your new pet hamster.

47096479R00028